D1447400

Karma and Reincarnation

Karma and Reincarnation

Paramhansa Yogananda

Crystal Clarity Publishers
Nevada City, California

Crystal Clarity Publishers, Nevada City, CA 95959
Copyright © 2007 Hansa Trust
All rights reserved

Printed in China 2013
ISBN13: 978-1-56589-216-3
ePub ISBN13: 978-1-56589-609-3

Designed by Crystal Clarity Publishers

Library of Congress Cataloging-in-Publication Data
Yogananda, Paramhansa, 1893-1952.
Karma, and Reincarnation / by Paramhansa Yogananda.
p. cm. — (Wisdom of Yogananda ; 2)
ISBN-13: 978-1-56589-216-3 (trade paper, indexed)
1. Self-Realization Fellowship. 2. Karma. 3. Death. 4. Reincarnation.
I. Title. II. Series.
BP605.S4Y56 2006
294.5'23—dc22

2006024945

www.crystalclarity.com
800-424-1055
clarity@crystalclarity.com

Contents

Publisher's Note

Dear Reader,

Karma, death, and reincarnation are fascinating subjects for many of us. The more we understand them, the richer and more meaningful life becomes for us. In this book you'll read the words of Paramhansa Yogananda, a great master of yoga who wrote not from speculation, but from his inner perception of truth.

Yogananda offered teachings that can fill your life with inspiration and clarify your spiritual direction.

Paramhansa Yogananda came to the United States from India in 1920, bringing to the West the teachings and techniques of yoga, the ancient science of soul awakening. He was the first master of yoga to make his home in the West, and his *Autobiography of a Yogi* has become the bestselling spiritual autobiography of all time, awakening fascination in Westerners with the spiritual teachings of the East.

Yoga is the ancient science of redirecting one's energies inward to produce spiritual awakening. In addition to bringing Americans the most practical and effective techniques of meditation, Yogananda showed how these principles can be applied to all areas of life. He was a prolific writer, lecturer, and composer. He lived in America thirty-two years, until his death in 1952.

The articles included in this book are taken from several sources: the lessons he wrote in the 1920s and 1930s; articles of his that appeared in *Inner Culture* and *East West* magazines, published before 1943; the 1946 edition of *Autobiography of a Yogi*; Yogananda's original interpretation of *The Rubaiyat of Omar Khayyam*, edited by Swami Kriyananda; and notes taken by Swami Kriyananda during the years he lived with Yogananda as a close disciple.

Our goal in this book is to let the Master's spirit come clearly through, with a minimum of editing. Sometimes sentences, redundant in the present context, have been deleted. Sometimes words or punctuation have been changed to clarify the meaning. Most of what is included here is not available elsewhere.

May Yogananda's words on this important subject bring you understanding, comfort, and inspiration.

Crystal Clarity Publishers

Karma and Reincarnation

Chapter 1

The Law of Karma

What Is Karma?

If we accept the principle of cause and effect in Nature, and of action and reaction in physics, how can we not believe that this natural law extends also to human beings? Once consciousness is understood as basic to everything the question begs to be asked: Do not humans, too, belong to the natural order?

Such is the law of karma: As you sow, so shall you reap.* If you sow evil, you will reap evil in the form of suffering. And if you sow goodness, you will reap goodness in the form of inner joy.

To understand karma, you must realize that thoughts are things. The very universe, in the final analysis, is composed not of matter but of consciousness. Matter responds, far more than most people realize, to the power of thought. For will power directs energy, and energy in turn acts upon matter. Matter, indeed, *is* energy.

Every action, every thought, reaps its own corresponding rewards.

* "Be not deceived; God is not mocked: for whatsoever a man soweth, that shall he also reap." *(Galatians 6:7)*

Human suffering is not a sign of God's, or Nature's, anger with mankind. It is a sign, rather, of man's ignorance of the divine law.

The law is forever infallible in its workings.

The Soul Is Free

Souls are "made" in the image of God. Even the greatest of all sinners cannot be damned forever. A finite cause cannot have an infinite effect. Due to the misuse of his free will, a person might imagine himself to be evil, but within he is a son of God. A king's son might, under the influence of liquor or of a bad dream, think himself poor, but as soon as he recovers from his state of intoxication, or as soon as he awakens, he forgets that delusion. The perfect soul, ever sinless, eventually wakes up in God when it remembers its real, eternally good, nature.

Man, being made in the image of God, is deluded only temporarily. This temporary delusion leads him to think of himself as mortal. So long as he identifies with mortality he must suffer.

A soul's delusion of mortality may extend to many incarnations. Through self-effort, however, always influenced by the law of God, the Prodigal Son develops discrimination, remembers his home in God, and attains wisdom. With illumination the prodigal soul remembers its eternal image of God, and is reunited with cosmic consciousness. His Father then serves him "the fatted calf" of eternal bliss and wisdom, liberating him forever.

Delusion Is Temporary

Man may misuse his free will for a time, considering himself mortal, but that temporary delusion can never erase from within him the mark of immortality and God's image of perfection. A baby's premature death cannot possibly have permitted him the use of free will to be either virtuous or vicious. Nature must bring that soul back to earth to give it a chance to use its free will to work out also the past karma which caused it to die so young, and to perform the good actions that lead to liberation.

If an immortal soul has not worked out in one lifetime of school those delusions which bind him, he needs more lifetimes of schooling to bring him the understanding of his innate immortality. Only then can he return to the state of cosmic consciousness. Ordinary souls therefore reincarnate, compelled by their earth-bound desires. Great souls, on the other hand, come on earth only partly to work out their karma, but principally to act as noble sons of God to show lost children the way to their heavenly Father's home.

Attracting a Bodily Home

When good parents unite in physical union, they produce a pure astral light as the positive and negative currents at the base of their spines and in their sex organs, unite. This light is a signal to good souls with compatible vibrations in the astral world to be physically conceived in the union of the sperm and ovum cells. When the soul enters, the embryo is formed, and the body is gradually made ready to be born.

Souls with bad karma have to enter into the body of evil mothers. When evil parents come into physical union, they form a dim, impure light at the base of the spine, signaling an invitation to souls with evil karma.

Like attracts like. Souls with evil karma are born into evil families; souls with good karma are born into good families. Evil families and good families attract souls according to the magnetism of their inner likings. That is, evil families attract souls with bad karma. Good families attract good souls. The attraction is based on mutual likes and dislikes. Evil entities have an affinity for evil families, whereas the affinity of good souls is for good families.

People with more opportunity in life, owing to their good karma, should help those with lesser opportunity, otherwise they'll develop bad karma. Selfishness is spiritually degrading and ultimately makes one unfortunate.

God is not a divine autocrat passing judgment on people for their actions. The judgments of cosmic law are based on karmic cause and effect, and are just.

The divine law of harmony creates a natural equilibrium. When any soul acts against this equilibrium, he hurts himself. For example, if you dip your hand in cool water you enjoy a soothing sensation, but if you approach fire, the very heat of it warns you that your hand may get burnt. The fire has no will to give you pain, nor does cool water produce a pleasant sensation out of choice. The responsibility for getting burnt by fire is his who puts his hand into it. And the responsibility for feeling pleasure from cool water is, again, his who inserts his hand into the water. Fire and water, heat and coolness, are part of the overall state of the universe with which our duty is to live in harmony.

We Punish Ourselves

By wrong living one can create a physical and mental hell even worse than the fiery hell that vengeful people imagine for others after death. By good living one can create within himself a place even sweeter than the heaven people imagine for themselves in the after-death state.

Man, influenced by delusion, ascribes to the all-loving God a vindictive spirit that creates hells and purgatories. God, in his infinite love, is calling the soul continuously to come back to His eternal kingdom of Bliss. But souls, when they misuse their God-given independence, wander away from God and wallow in the mire of suffering, punishing themselves by the effects of their own errors.

The idea of an eternal heaven is true, though most people's ideas of heaven are very limited. We are made in the image of God and, at the end of the long trail of incarnations, our wandering actuated by material desires, we will find the blissful heavenly Father waiting to receive us, His prodigal children, and to entertain us with everlasting, ever-new joy. But the idea of eternal damnation for souls made in the image of God is untenable and should be exploded and banished as a superstition from the minds of men.

Good Karma

This life is like a movie, and just like in an exciting movie, there has to be a villain so we will learn to love the hero. If you imitate the villain's behavior, however, you will receive his punishment. It's all a dream, but ask yourselves, Why live a bad dream by creating bad karma? With good karma, you get to enjoy the dream. Good karma also makes you want, in time, to wake up from the dream. Bad karma, on the other hand, darkens the mind and keeps it bound to the dreaming process.

From a mountaintop, one sees clearly the whole countryside, and also the open sky above. From the heights it is natural to want to soar even higher, far above the earth. In the fog-bound valley below, however, the most that one aspires to may be only to climb a little bit higher.

Evil Karma and "Hell-fire"

The Heavenly Father could not possibly send his human children to hell forever for making mistakes during their brief sojourn on earth. When they misuse their God-given independence, they must suffer the material consequences of their *own* evil actions, and reward themselves through their own good karma or virtuous deeds.

Those humans who act wrongly create evil tendencies, which remain hidden in the brain ready to pour out fiery suffering at a suitable time. These hidden, misery-making tendencies—or hell-fires—are carried into the astral world at death by a soul with bad karma. Souls in the after-death state have no physical sensations and could not be burned by physical fire. But souls with bad karma can suffer mental agonies worse than fiery burns.

The word "hell" is from the Anglo-Saxon root "*helan*, to conceal." The Greek root is "*helios*, sun or fire." Therefore, the word "hell-fire" is very appropriate to depict the concealed fire of agony that stored-up tendencies can produce in one's earthly life or in the astral world. Just as a murderer burns with evil conscience during wakefulness and with subconscious terror during sleep, so he suffers from fiery evils in the sleep state of death.

A benign father could never eternally burn a soul made in His own image for its temporary mistakes on earth. The idea of eternal punishment is illogical. A soul is forever made in the image of God. Even a million years of sin could not change its essential, divine character. Man's unforgiving wrath against the evil actions of his brethren has created this misconception of eternal hell-fire.

My Experience with an Orthodox Believer

Once I met an old man who lived near Seattle. I had been sitting near the sea, much inspired by the vastness of divinity. After that inspiration subsided I felt hungry, and went to the farmhouse of this man, seeking to buy some cherries. The rosy-cheeked man looked very happy, and showed me kind hospitality. A divine impulse then came over me, and I said to him, "Friend, you look happy, but there is a hidden suffering in your life." He asked, "Are you a fortune-teller?" I answered, "No, but I tell people how to improve their fortunes."

He then said, "We are all sinners, and the Lord will burn our souls in hell-fire and brimstone."

I replied, "How could a man, losing his body at death and becoming an invisible soul, be burned by fire created by material brimstones?" He surprised me by repeating angrily, "We will certainly burn in hell-fire." I said, "Did you get a telegram about this from God, that He will burn us in hell-fire?" At this the old man became even more agitated.

To mollify him, I changed the subject and said, "What about your unhappiness over your wicked son?" He was surprised at my words and acknowledged that he was helpless to correct his son, whom he deemed incorrigible. This sorrow remained as a burning fire at the back of his mind.

I said, "I have a remedy that will absolutely cure this situation." The old man's eyes gleamed with joy as he smiled. I, then, with a mysterious attitude as if about to reveal the grand solution, whispered to him, "Have you got a very big oven with a broiler?"

"Why, yes," he said. Then, suspiciously he asked, "Just what are you getting at?"

"Don't worry," I said reassuringly. "What I'm proposing will end all your sorrows."

Somewhat mollified, he said, "Go on."

"Now then," I continued, "Heat that oven, with the broiler, to red-hot temperature. Do you have some strong rope and two trusted friends who would not repeat anything against you?" Again he said, "Why, yes." Then I said, "Call your son here. With the help of your friends, bind him hand and foot, and slip him into the red-hot oven."

The old man was furious! Shaking his fist at me, he shouted, "You blackguard! Who ever heard of a father burning his son, no matter how wicked?"

I then spoke soothingly, "That is exactly what I wanted to tell you. Where did you, who are human, get this instinct of love except from the Divine Father? Even a human father cannot stand the cruel thought of roasting his own son alive to put him, or himself, out of misery. How could you think the Divine Father, who has infinitely greater love than you, and who created parental love, would burn His own children with hell-fire and brimstone?"

The old man's eyes filled with tears of repentance as he said, "I understand now that the Heavenly Father is a God of love!"

We punish ourselves by our own evil actions, and reward ourselves by our own good deeds.

Sin cannot change the soul. We, who are made in the image of God, can be lost in the jungles of an evil environment for a while, but no amount of sin can change our eternal, divine nature. Sin is a crust which hides the perfect soul, made eternally in the image of God. When that crust is dissolved by meditation, the perfection of the soul is revealed at last.

God Wants to Help Us

When God sees that a soul, by the misuse of free will and bad company, has lost itself in the forest of egotism, He becomes very concerned for him, and sends him spiritual aid to bring him back into His fold of divine, virtuous living. He helps souls to reincarnate in places where they can work out their karmas and liberate their souls by meditation and wisdom. All souls on earth belong to the fold of God; the Invisible Shepherd ever looks after them.

CHAPTER 2

HOW TO FACE YOUR KARMA*

* From *The Rubaiyat of Omar Khayyam Explained by Paramhansa Yogananda*, edited by Swami Kriyananda

Life Is a Game

The alternating nights and days of this rotating Earth, and the alternating sorrows and joys in people's lives, are like a checkerboard in multi-dimensions. The rules of the game are set by Karma, the law of cause and effect. Karma arranges the reunion of friends lost to one another in the dark night of death. Karma withdraws souls back into the astral world again, when their time on earth has expired.

As chess pieces, when "captured," are removed and placed in a box, so Destiny, when removing people from the "board" of life, places them in the secret "closet," or resting place, of the other world.

View life's ups and downs with a serene mind. For outward existence is only a game. View your wins and losses with mental detachment, as you would a movie. After viewing a good drama, even a tragic one, you exclaim, "What a good story! I learned much from it." Similarly, even after experiencing tragic events in your life, tell yourself, "I am grateful for that experience! It taught me much."

Life needs variety to be interesting. If a novel makes us laugh or cry, we appreciate it. Think of life as a good novel, or a good movie. Step back from it a little, mentally.

View it in perspective. If you don't like the plot, remember, the freer you are inside, the greater will be your ability to change it.

Karma rules. But who was it set our karma into motion? We did!

Whatever we did in the past we can undo. All we need now is the right determination, born of our increasing inner freedom.

People enjoy games such as chess, and accept their wins and losses more or less even-mindedly. In the same spirit, let us enjoy life, whether it gives us victory or defeat. Let us live calmly and with a sense of gratitude. In that spirit let us enjoy meeting true friends again—after who knows how many lives? And let us accept with calm faith our parting again at death.

Life is a game. Be interested in it, but remain always non-attached. Let nothing affect you inwardly. However things go, remember, there is nothing real about it. Don't be like a certain person who, exultant after winning a chess game, died of a heart attack!

Even during dark hours of bereavement, and during your body's inexorable descent into old age, keep a joyful attitude. The black squares on a checkerboard alternate with the white. Even so, every darkness in life alternates with light, every sorrow with a joy, every failure with a success. Change and contrast are inevitable, and are what make the great game possible. View them dispassionately, and never allow them to define who you are, inside.

Karma Is Our Own Responsibility

Man, in his soul, is not predestined to be either good or bad. While vice or virtue may seem inborn, every human tendency is self-acquired either in this life or in former lives. It is the result of individual choice.

To rationalize one's shortcomings by such claims as, "I am bad only because my karma makes me so," or, "Satan pushed me; it is *his* fault, not mine," is to reason dangerously. Unfortunately, many people take this line of argument. Somewhere, they hope, hidden in the vast, crowded warehouse of their past experiences, there must exist some good excuse: some long-forgotten sin committed not *by* them, but *against* them, some influence before the power of which they were but victims.

In modern times, with psychoanalysis a subject of widespread fascination, people are conditioned to blame their problems on others' treatment of them—on the cruelty or indifference of parents, teachers, society—anything, to avoid having to face the need to improve themselves.

It is mere subterfuge on the ego's part to plead helplessness in the face of difficulties. The root causes of our problems grow out of sight, in the subconscious. We put down those roots *ourselves*, originally, by wrong deeds that we performed in the past. Today, if anyone behaves badly toward us, it is him we blame for our hurt. That we might in some way have *attracted* that hurt never enters our minds. If our "luck" turns against us, *we* blame anything and anyone but ourselves. Yet it is we, by the magnetism projected by our own karma, who drew that hurtful behavior, or that "rotten luck," to ourselves.

Every circumstance in our lives, every characteristic, every habit, however much we now repudiate it, was something we ourselves created, whether recently or in the distant past. Each one is due to our misuse of the free choice God first bestowed on us.

He gave us the freedom to return to Him, if we so decided, or to allow our lives to flow futilely toward sense-indulgences. From Him, the only Source of life, flow all strength and goodness. If our life force flows outward continually, alienating itself from its Divine Source within, it enters an arid desert. In barren sands of matter-consciousness, its streams become absorbed and disappear.

Blame no one for the evils that beset you. Accept responsibility for your own life, and for whatever misfortunes you encounter. Do your best, with firm resolution, to eliminate the harmful tendencies in your own nature.

Above all, go back to God.

Only by perfect self-honesty and dynamic self-effort will you eliminate forever the influence of satanic delusion in your life. Remember, it was you who invited that influence, by your own thoughts and actions. Live from today onward guided by divine wisdom from within.

How to Handle Karmic Challenges

People seldom look for hidden causes behind the occurrences in their lives. They cannot understand why they suffer. Suffering itself draws a thick curtain over their minds, obscuring its origins.

Only through deep, inner communion with higher states of consciousness does it become clear that all deficiencies, whether mental or physical, are the just consequences of a person's misbehavior in the past. A wise sage has the inner clarity to perceive the exact cause of every mishap. He can then prescribe actions that will remove that cause as an influence in a person's life.

One who was born disadvantaged in any way should resist fiercely the temptation to wallow in self-pity. To feel sorry for oneself is but to dilute one's inner power to overcome. Instead, affirm, "There are no obstacles: There are only *opportunities*!"

Accuse no one, not even yourself. Blame and accusation won't erase what has been done; it will affirm, rather, your dependency on circumstances over which, truly, you have lost control.

Seek God in the inner silence. Reconcile yourself to what is, and to what needs to be done about it. You can re-shape every karma, provided that from today onward you live by soul-consciousness. Repudiate the dictates of your ego. They are forever grounded in delusion.

The closer you come to God, the more surely you will know Him as Divine Love itself: the Nearest of the near, the very Dearest of the dear.

Living from Within Leads to Freedom from Karma

Most human beings refuse to be guided from within, by higher wisdom. Instead, they live influenced by the deeply entrenched habits they created in the past. Their lives, in consequence, are like balls struck at the player's whim. As the ball in a game must go where it is sent, so mankind, habit-driven, has no choice but to live out the results of his karma as dictated by his own former actions

Most human beings are slaves to their conditioning, which may appear as an outward cause but in fact has its origin within themselves. They are controlled by their habits. Although those habits were created initially by themselves, a habit, once formed, is self-perpetuating.

Very few people have any idea how insidiously their action-generated habits of the past influence their present behavior, their mental outlook, the companions and environment they attract, and what they mistakenly call their "luck," whether good or bad. They cannot see those habits welling up from deep in the subconscious mind, nor how they silently affect all their present attitudes and actions. People—Westerners, especially—believe they have free will. Others—mostly Easterners—imagine just as erroneously that there is no way out, that all is Kismet: Fate.

But there is a way out! That way is to renounce the false notion that we demonstrate freedom by giving free reign to our egoic desires. In Karma's realm, Karma rules supreme. Yet human beings have the power to withdraw to another realm altogether, by attuning themselves with the infinite wisdom behind karmic law. This much freedom is ours eternally: to accept God and His guidance from within, or to continue to be guided by our egoic desires.

The more we live guided from within, the greater our control over outer events in the great game of life. For when we live at our own center, in superconsciousness, we live in the only true freedom there is. In soul-consciousness we are no longer helplessly controlled by habits and desires. To the extent, then, that we develop soul-consciousness, we free ourselves from karmic slavery.

Instead of accepting fatalistically the decrees of karma, follow the inner way to freedom. Meditate daily. Commune deeply with God. Learn from Him, through the silent voice of intuition, the way out of soul-degrading serfdom to habits.

How long—how tragically long!—have habits kept you fearful about the future. If unexpected fortune and misfortune in your life confuse you, seek the only solution there is to life's endless puzzle: deep meditation, and increasing attunement with wisdom through daily contact with the ever-free, Infinite Spirit.

Transcending Ego

Karma's unalterable decrees govern human destiny only as long as man continues to live through his senses, in reaction to outer events. For such a person, moral reasoning is centered in ego-consciousness. Scriptural learning is centered in ego-consciousness. Self-pitying tears are centered in ego-consciousness. Ego-consciousness is the problem. The greater its hold on the mind, the greater karma's hold on our lives.

Cosmic Law is no irrational tyrant, however. Its judgments are not inflicted mindlessly on a cowering and helpless humanity. Every consequence ordained by Divine Law is right and just; it springs from deeper realities in human nature itself, and is meted out for deeds already committed. Is it not reasonable, indeed, that we reap the just results of our own actions?

Once the ego has been transcended in soul-consciousness, however, the realm of karmic law is transcended also. The soul remains forever unaffected, for karmic consequences accrue only to the ego. They are dissipated when no centripetal vortex is left to bring them to a focus in the consciousness of "I" and "mine."

In Self-realization, the soul is released at last from its bondage to karmic law. Even the good actions performed by great saints spread outward, like ripples of light, in blessing to all mankind.

Chapter 3
Freedom from Karma

Overcoming Karma

Once upon a time a powerful emperor of a country got drunk. Disguised, he went into a tavern belonging to his estate and in a quarrel broke another man's leg. The innkeeper took him to a judge who had been appointed to his post by the king. As the judge was about to pass sentence, the king suddenly threw off his disguise and exclaimed, "I am the king who appointed you as the judge, and I have the power to throw you into prison. How dare you convict me?"

In a similar way, the perfect soul, when it is identified with the body, may commit an evil and be deemed guilty according to the judge—or law of karma. But when that soul can identify its consciousness with God, the Creator of the law of karma, that royal soul cannot be punished by the judging law.

One can escape the law of karma by identifying himself with God. Once he is able to do that, he should forgive his brothers who sin against him. But if that soul, who found divine forgiveness from his own karma by meditation, is unforgiving toward his sinning brothers, then he again identifies with human life and becomes governed by the inscrutable laws of limiting karma. Every soul, therefore, should remain divine by continuously forgiving and loving as God does.

According to the laws of a country, a judge may sentence a young criminal to three years in a reformatory school. But the judge also has the privilege to pardon the young offender if the youth repents and promises to behave well in future. So, according to the law of karma, a person who acts evilly must reap the consequences of his actions. But if that evildoer appeals to God for pardon by intense prayer and meditation, then God, being the Maker of the law of karma, can grant him amnesty from punishment.

The Consciousness of Great Souls

Most souls, when entering this world, are not consciously in control of their own destinies. Dimly they understand that the flow of their desires brings them here. Beyond this murky awareness, however, they have no sense of purpose or direction.

Advanced souls are not so limited. They know why they have come, and what they have to do on earth. In attunement with God's will and with inner, soul guidance, they direct their lives and the lives of others toward ever-greater freedom in the Infinite.

Others, too, as they learn to contact the ever-new joy in meditation, rise gradually above gross matter-consciousness into the freedom of Spirit.

The clearer the soul's awareness of higher guidance, the greater its freedom from the dictates of karma. Perfect surrender to God's will is not in any way passive. Great will power and great concentration are needed to attune the mind perfectly. Surrender enables the soul to expand its consciousness, like a boundless sphere of light, until it encompasses omnipresence. Blissful soul-expansion brings with it increasing dominion—not only over one's own self, but over all matter.

Kriya Yoga and Freedom from Karma

"Kriya Yoga is an instrument through which human evolution can be quickened." Sri Yukteswar explained to his students. . . .*

The life of an advanced Kriya Yogi is influenced, not by effects of past actions, but solely by directions from the soul. The devotee thus avoids the slow, evolutionary monitors of egoistic actions, good and bad, of common life, cumbrous and snail-like to the eagle hearts. . . .

Identifying himself with a shallow ego, man takes for granted that it is he who thinks, wills, feels, digests meals, and keeps himself alive, never admitting through reflection (only a little would suffice!) that in his ordinary life he is naught but a puppet of past actions (karma) and of nature or environment. Each man's intellectual reactions, feelings, moods, and habits are circumscribed by effects of past causes, whether of this or a prior life. Lofty above such influences, however, is his regal soul. . . .

The advanced yogi, withholding all his mind, will, and feeling from false identification with bodily desires, uniting

*More information on Kriya Yoga and Sri Yukteswar can be found in *Autobiography of a Yogi* by Paramhansa Yogananda.

his mind with superconscious forces in the spinal shrines, thus lives in this world as God hath planned, not impelled by impulses from the past nor by new witlessnesses of fresh human motivations. Such a yogi receives fulfillment of his Supreme Desire, safe in the final haven of inexhaustibly blissful Spirit.

The Masters Take On the Karma of Others

Fortunately for his disciples, Sri Yukteswar burned many of their sins in the fire of his severe fever in Kashmir. The metaphysical method of physical transfer of disease is known to highly advanced yogis. A strong man can assist a weaker one by helping to carry his heavy load; a spiritual superman is able to minimize his disciples' physical or mental burdens by sharing the karma of their past actions. Just as a rich man loses some money when he pays off a large debt for his prodigal son, who is thus saved from dire consequences of his own folly, so a master willingly sacrifices a portion of his bodily wealth to lighten the misery of disciples.

By a secret method, the yogi unites his mind and astral vehicle with those of a suffering individual; the disease is conveyed, wholly or in part, to the saint's body. Having harvested God on the physical field, a master no longer cares what happens to that material form. Though he may allow it to register a certain disease in order to relieve others, his mind is never affected; he considers himself fortunate in being able to render such aid.

The devotee who has achieved final salvation in the Lord finds that his body has completely fulfilled its purpose; he can then use it in any way he deems fit. His work in the world is to alleviate the sorrows of mankind, whether through spiritual means or by intellectual counsel or through will power or by the physical transfer of disease. Escaping to the superconsciousness whenever he so desires, a master can remain oblivious of physical suffering; sometimes he chooses to bear bodily pain stoically, as an example to disciples. By putting on the ailments of others, a yogi can satisfy, for them, the karmic law of cause and effect. This law is mechanically or mathematically operative; its workings can be scientifically manipulated by men of divine wisdom.

The spiritual law does not require a master to become ill whenever he heals another person. Healings ordinarily take place through the saint's knowledge of various methods of instantaneous cure in which no hurt to the spiritual healer is involved. On rare occasions, however, a master who wishes to greatly quicken his disciples' evolution may then voluntarily work out on his own body a large measure of their undesirable karma.

Jesus signified himself as a ransom for the sins of many. With his divine powers, his body could never have been subjected to death by crucifixion if he had not willingly cooperated with the subtle cosmic law of cause and effect. He thus took on himself the consequences of others' karma, especially that of his disciples. In this manner they were highly purified and made fit to receive the omnipresent consciousness which later descended on them.

Only a self-realized master can transfer his life force, or convey into his own body the diseases of others. An ordinary man cannot employ this yogic method of cure, nor is it desirable that he should do so; for an unsound physical instrument is a hindrance to God-meditation. The Hindu scriptures teach that the first duty of man is to keep his body in good condition; otherwise his mind is unable to remain fixed in devotional concentration.

THE IMPORTANCE OF MEDITATION

Who would not like a reprieve from the consequences of his own wrong deeds? Few people, however, are willing to do what is necessary to win such a reprieve. For it is not pleading that can free us from the grinding wheel of justice. Cosmic Law is mathematical in its precision. The way to escape its decrees is to live in divine consciousness. Freedom comes not by uttering wheedling prayers, but by attuning oneself deeply with the all-loving Inner Silence.

No matter how busy we are with our work or with worldly affairs, we should strive in the inner silence to attune ourselves with God. By silent devotion we can deepen our awareness of divine love and wisdom. The Divine is above the law. In everything we do, we should feel God's all-creative Intelligence working through us. The closer we live to God, the less His law will be able to affect us.

The greatest "business" of all is to busy ourselves with God. The greatest duty of all is to place Him first in our lives. No business and no earthly duty would be possible without the intelligence man derives from Him.

Make it a point always to keep your most important of all engagements: your daily appointment with the Lord.

Twice daily, enter the inner silence. Worship God on the altar of the dawn. At the day's end, sit quietly in the temple of the night; let darkness conceal you from the distractions of the day.

Contemplate the monotonous recurrence of death and rebirth. While still in this body, work to destroy the seeds of your past karmas (actions). Remember, roasted seeds will not germinate. People who in deep meditation roast their karmic seeds in the fires of wisdom will never again need to reincarnate on earth.

Chapter 4
Death and Resurrection

What Happens at Death?

When the ordinary person approaches death, usually his whole body becomes paralyzed, just as a part of your body sometimes "goes to sleep." When your foot goes to sleep, you see it and you know that it is yours, but you cannot move or use it. So, at the approach of death, most people feel an entire paralysis, or a going-to-sleep state of the entire body—limbs, muscles, and even internal organs, including heart, lungs, and diaphragm.

In the beginning, the dying man is conscious of the slow falling asleep of the muscles and limbs. When the heart begins to grow numb, there is a sense of suffocation, because without heart action the lungs cannot operate. This sense of suffocation is a little painful for about one to three seconds, and causes a great fear of death. Because souls reincarnate many times, and necessarily have to experience death in passing from an old body into the body of a little child, they retain the memory of this feeling of suffocation and pain at death. This memory of pain causes fear of death.

Physical and Psychological States at Death

The ordinary man, at the time of death, experiences the following sensations:

1. Gradual numbness of the limbs, muscles, heart, lungs, and diaphragm.

2. During the spreading of numbness in the limbs and muscles, a sense of sadness, helplessness, and a desire to live, comes into the mind.

3. When the numbness reaches the heart muscles, a sense of pain and suffocation is experienced which causes an extreme fear of death. An attachment toward possessions and loved ones strongly comes upon the soul and causes extreme mental grief.

4. With the pain of suffocation, there is a great mental struggle to bring the breath back again. At this time, a condensed review of all the good and bad actions of his lifetime comes up in the mind of the dying man. From this mental introspection comes the guiding tendency in determining the kind of birth the dying man will have in the next life.

5. At this time, the senses of touch, taste, smell, sight, and hearing vanish in succession. The sense of

hearing is the last to leave the consciousness of the dying man. That is why it is extremely unwise even to whisper within the hearing of a dying person: "All is over; he is about to die."

Two students of mine, a brother and sister, had a singular experience. The sister lay dying in a room, with her brother and doctors in attendance. When the brother left the room for a moment to get some water, the doctors exclaimed: "All is over; her pulse has failed." There was a spasm and she lay apparently dead. As soon as the brother came back, he ordered everybody out of the room. He then shook his sister vigorously, crying: "Sister, your teacher told you to make the effort and you will live."

In a few moments her pulse came back; she breathed, sat up, and told the following experience: "My entire body was paralyzed, but I could hear the footsteps of my brother leaving the room. I was making an effort to stir the life force in my inert body by will, but as soon as I heard the doctors say: 'All is over,' I gave up the will to live and I witnessed a complete inertia in my outer muscles and internal organs, and a blinding flash of light in the head, followed by intense darkness. In this state, I heard my brother coming toward me as though from afar, and as soon as he urged me to use my will power and wake up, I revived my will to live, and here I am. My consciousness was able to resuscitate itself into the inner organs, muscles, and the senses, which had become inert before."

Since the last predominating thought of a dying person is weighted down with the habit tendency of a lifetime, it is not good to overburden this consciousness with the fear of death.

The dying man should be told nothing, or, if he is a brave man and wants to die, whisper into his ear: "Cross the portal of this woeful life into the vista of everlasting happiness."

6. The ordinary person, after he experiences the sense of suffocation, finds himself suddenly relieved of the weight of his body, of the necessity of breathing, and of any physical pain.
7. After that, the soul of the dead man enters into a state of oblivious sleep a million times deeper and more enjoyable than the state of ordinary deep sleep.

8. A sense of soaring through a very peaceful, dark tunnel is experienced by the soul.
9. Sometimes, when a man dies quickly, for instance by hanging or electrocution, or from a shot or sudden accident, he experiences practically no physical pain.

The suffering is purely mental, when the mind realizes it cannot breathe or live again in that body. An imaginary sense of suffocation and pain at death turns into a painful mental nightmare, which for some time tortures the mental feeling of the dead man, but after a little while, when the soul realizes that its body is gone, it becomes reconciled. If a good soul is murdered, he seldom suffers even mental agony after a sudden death.

The Astral Body Becomes the Base of Operation After Death

Though the physical body is a dream of God, still it seems real when it is possessed by the ego. Likewise, the astral body in death seems real and becomes the base of operation for the ego. As the physical body can have human dreams, so also the astral body (after the death of the physical body) can create any dream within itself.

Saints and men of concentration who, during their earthly existence, have practiced the technique of meditation, can retain their consciousness even when the heart slows down or stops; they are eligible to retain their consciousness during the state of deathly sleep. Just as we can enjoy a deep sleep, or watch the working of a beautiful dream semi-consciously, so also, in conscious death all astral experiences are watched consciously or semi-consciously.

Astral Climate

The astral cosmos is more naturally attuned than the earth to the divine will and plan of perfection. Every astral object is manifested primarily by the will of God, and partially by the will-call of astral beings. They possess the power of modifying or enhancing the grace and form of anything already created by the Lord.

The astral land appears to the soul as a very beautiful garden. Here he finds an astral climate evenly hot and cold, capable of being controlled by the power of the will, just as modern people can warm or cool their homes by means of electric heat or air conditioning.

There is astral winter, spring, rainy season, and summer. The astral winter consists of exquisitely beautiful, cool but not cold, white fleecy clouds, or rays, floating over the astral land. The astral snow is ordered by the inhabitants, mostly to decorate the scenery. This snow changes the temperature according to the will of the astral inhabitants.

The astral spring and summer are filled with an infinite variety of celestial blossoms smiling on the soil of transparent, frozen, golden light. The flowers blossom and change, or vanish, with an endless variety of blended colors, according to the fancy of the astral gardener. Flowers never die. They only vanish or change when they are no longer wanted.

In the astral rainy season, the rays pour down over the golden soil, emanating an ineffable variety of music of the spheres. They form flower shapes as they fall, so that during the astral rain one can perceive a sheet of silver threads dangling daisies and roses of light, and showering them on the astral land. Flower-shaped pools of light bedeck the streets during an astral rain.

Astral Houses

In the astral land there are many mansions or spheres of various multi-colored luminous vibrations. Just as the city has different neighborhoods—the wealthy and the slum districts—so the astral kingdom has many quarters of different kinds of dwellings. The astral abodes are made of bricks composed of condensed atoms.

The saints live in the refined astral realms. Here ordinary souls would freeze to death or suffocate, but the saints can live in extreme cold or extreme warmth, free from magnetic disturbances. Wicked souls live in the astral slums, and are unable to enter the refined atmosphere of the blessed spiritual aristocrats.

Reincarnation in the Astral Land

There is birth and death and reincarnation in the astral land, just as there is in earth life, only in the astral land life is very long and death, or change, is not forced upon any advanced soul—the wicked astral souls excepted.

When the advanced soul lovingly remembers earthly experiences, it may have to go back again and experience life and death in the physical world. The astral death has no pain or fear.

Astral Diseases and Crime

Astral diseases consist mostly in mental moods and mental defects, or astral malnutrition. These astral diseases are easily remedied by the powerful minds of almost all astral inhabitants.

Astral crime consists in ignorance and in seeking selfish happiness. There are no judges to punish anyone. Souls punish themselves when they are wrong, by self-imposed discipline.

How Can We Get in Touch with the Dead?

Do not try to contact tramp souls who infest the ether with their presence. As tramps can occupy and ruin an empty, unlocked automobile, so tramp souls can get into absentminded, shallow-minded people who try to invoke spirits through a passive state of mind. These tramp souls can possess the brain and wreck it. That is why people who passively allow themselves to be possessed usually lose their character, mind, and spiritual power.

Only true souls who loved you, and who continue to love you, should be invited. You need good souls to help you, and you can also send them help.

How to Invite Good Souls

Concentrate deeply, with patience, until you can see your spiritual eye (a silver-white star in an opal-blue field encased in a golden aureole) with closed and open eyes. You must be able to retain this as long as you want. Then visualize the good soul you want to meet, and constantly invite him to come into the light. If you have patience and strong personal zeal, you will see and speak to that image, as in a talking picture, on the screen of the spiritual eye. By deeper development, you will be able to see that soul with open eyes.

If a soul like Jesus accepts your invitation, he can be not only visible to you, but can also vibrate his body grossly so that you can also hear him and touch him.

Bad souls cannot enter the entrenched, highly electrified orb of the spiritual eye. Only good souls who can help you can make themselves visible in the spiritual eye.

How to Drive Bad Spirits Away

If someone else is possessed by a bad spirit, touch his forehead with the forefinger of your right hand and put the forefinger of your left hand over the medulla; then press on both hands, look through your own spiritual eye, and say: "By the astral light I scorch thee, and command thee to get out."

If you yourself are thus troubled, before going to sleep write "AUM" or "Amen" on your pillow with your fingers. Mentally visualize light around your body, look into the spiritual eye and say several times, mentally or loudly: "I am Light. Darkness fly away." Also, standing or sitting, touch both of your palms in front of your body, and then swing them to touch behind your back, and then forward again several times in rapid succession, chanting "AUM," and you will be protected.

Contacting Departed Souls

In real communication with a spirit, one should not lose consciousness, but should consciously commune with the invited soul. These states are usually devoid of exciting emotions. Do not try quick, magic tricks to get in touch with departed souls. That is a great spiritual crime against God and humanity. By deep, incessant meditation only, try to get in touch with your dear dead ones. Only meditation, and months, sometimes years, of patience can bring them to you.

Every night, with closed eyes, concentrate in the Christ Center, the astral broadcasting microphone of the spiritual eye, and send your good will to your departed ones by mentally saying: "Resurrect, and be quickened in God." They will get your message. Then sit in silence and try to feel their love; when you feel exhilarated, know that they have answered you.

Even if some of your dead loved ones have reincarnated, by the above process you can contact their ever-awake astral bodies and receive an answer in the form of a dream during sleep, or a vision during meditation.

By finding friends in this life and following them up in the astral sphere after death, you will learn the mystery of life after death. Then you will know that death separated your loved ones from you so that you might love not only them, but that you might give your love to all the people in all incarnations. When your heart becomes big enough to love all, you will then know the Father who loves all His children alike. Knowing Him, you will know all your many parents and friends that you loved before. With that intense love you will learn to love all your animate and inanimate brothers as children of your one, ever-kind, ever-mysterious Father-God.

Do not think constantly about a departed soul unless you know that he is good, and unless you feel an undying desire to reach him. If time cannot make you forget a departed friend, then try to contact him. A continuous desire to know about a departed soul is the best astral broadcasting that you can send forth.

Feeling Contact in the Conscious State

If, day and night, you miss a dear friend, then you will have a sort of longing, a soothing presence around your heart. This will indicate to you that this friendly soul is trying to get in touch with you through your feeling, but he cannot materialize himself because of your constant mental restlessness.

Dream Contact in the Subconscious State

If you concentrate upon the feeling that your friend is present for several minutes just before falling asleep, then that friend will appear to you in a dream.

Conscious Contact in the Superconscious State

If you carry the feeling of the presence of your departed friend, and then concentrate with closed eyes at the spot between the eyebrows and visualize him, he will appear to you after some time. It may take months, or even years, but if you are patient and keep on ever increasing the depth of the astral call of meditation, you will succeed.

The Metaphysical Technique of Finding Lost, Dearly Loved Friends

When you lose someone very dear to you by death and you find it impossible to forget him, then proceed to find him in the following way, practicing for two hours each day, for months—or, if necessary, for years: Sit on a straight chair, and practice the highest technique of concentration that you know for one hour; then lift your hand and concentrate on the finger tips. Concentrate on the point between the eyebrows, see the spiritual eye, and continuously will to contact the astral body of the departed soul.

Keep on turning your hand very gently in a circle toward all the different directions: north, south, east, and west, and so on. At every direction in the circle around which your hand moves, try to feel the presence of the astral body of the departed soul. When your fingers feel that you have touched him as you used to touch him while he lived, your heart will be thrilled. Keep on visualizing him in the spiritual eye and you will see him. Ask your fingers and heart to indicate in what place your friend is reborn, according to the direction you felt him through your fingers. When you feel him through your fingers and heart, and can see him and talk to him, he will tell you where he is in the astral world, or the place where he is born. Then there will be great rejoicing.

Examples of Resurrection

Swami Kriyananda tells the following stories:

There was a certain man in Encinitas who sold real estate. His wife had been seriously ill for ninety days. When the man heard of Yogananda, who lived locally and who had healing powers, he went and asked him to pray for her. Yogananda prayed, but was told, for then, not to go to the woman's bedside. Shortly thereafter, to the husband's despair, the wife died.

Then only was Yogananda told in meditation to go to their home. On entering, he found some thirty people assembled, all of them grieving. The husband was by the woman's side, weeping and shaking her desperately. Yogananda calmly motioned him away, then placed one hand over the dead woman's forehead, the other one on her back, and began to invoke the Divine Power.

Five or ten minutes later, her body began to shake—"like a motor," as Yogananda described it later. Presently, a deep calmness stole upon her. Her heartbeat and breathing returned. She slowly opened her eyes. In them was a far-away expression, as though she had just returned from a long journey.

She was completely healed.

"During my 1935 visit to India," Yogananda told us, "I was walking down a street in Serampore, where my Guru lived, when I heard loud lamentations coming from a house. As it happened, this home belonged to the relative of a friend of mine. I went inside, and was told this relative had just died. His family were all weeping. I went to the body and prayed deeply over it. By God's grace, the man was restored to life."

Doctor Lewis told me many years later, "I once asked the Master, 'Did you enter that home because of your personal connection with the man? or was it because God told you to?'

"Yogananda at once replied, 'Oh, because God told me to. Otherwise, I would not have gone.'"

Heaven Is Waiting

Death is not annihilation. Death is a state of passive, involuntary relaxation brought on by accident, disease, or sorrow. The forcible and permanent disconnection of life current from the body is popularly called "death" or complete annihilation of life. In reality it is only a temporary state—it is not the end of things, but merely the transfer from the domain of changeable, ugly matter to the realm of infinite joy and multicolored lights.

Why not learn the method by which you can switch off the life current from the entire body through conscious will by the steady practice of meditation, and thus free the soul from the bondage of death? Just as electricity does not die when a light bulb breaks, so our real self is not destroyed at death but retires into the infinite, Omnipresent Self.

We experience this earth through the five senses of taste, touch, smell, hearing, and sight. Heaven is experienced through intuition. That is why it is necessary to meditate often and deeply because in meditation you develop the sixth sense, or intuition. We are not flesh; we are Spirit. There is a heaven awaiting you, and the only way to get there is by developing your intuition through intense prayer and meditation.

The Magic Carrot

In ancient days, there lived in India a woman with a very quarrelsome disposition. She was named Kalaha, which means "quarrel" in Bengali. Miss Kalaha started word-battles with anyone at the slightest pretext, and she could brook no performance of any good action.

Time went by, and Kalaha grew in her evil disposition and wickedness. At last, the Angel of Death cast her out of her body. Then her astral body began to descend the spiral stairway of gloom down into the deepest region of stygian darkness. She landed with a thud on the vapor-spitting floor of Hades. In agony and fright she shouted for mercy as she saw the Angel of Death leaving her in that dismal place, where sinful shadows live in torture and despair.

Somehow, attracted by the plaintive, intense noise of the wicked woman, Yama (the Angel of Death) returned and accosted her: "Please," he said, "can't you remember any good action which you performed during your earthly sojourn, so that I might parole you from this awful place you've landed due to your self-created errors?"

The wicked woman scratched her head for a while, and after a long inner search, she cried out, "O yes, your Majesty,

I do remember one kind act of mine. Once I had a bunch of carrots. I was about to eat them all when I found that one of them contained a worm, so I gave that wormy carrot to another person. I may have suggested that he eat only the good part and throw away the rest without killing the worm."

"That will do," replied Yama. He waved his hand and that carrot came floating through the air toward the sin-filled woman. Yama continued, "Wicked soul, grasp this carrot and hang onto it. Don't loosen your hold, and it will take you up to heaven."

The woman greedily seized the carrot and started her ascent heavenward. Seeing this, another sinner grasped her leg, and a second sinner grasped the leg of the first, and a third hung onto the legs of the second, until, gradually, a chain of one hundred sinners was suspended from the feet of the wicked woman. The magic carrot, with the wicked woman and the chain of one hundred sinners, began to rise toward heaven like a zooming rocket.

The wicked woman was overjoyed to find herself so easily freed from the hands of after-death justice. Then she felt a tug at her feet, looked down, and realized that a long chain of sinners was going heavenward with her. The realization that they were all benefiting from this free ride infuriated her. She couldn't bear the thought of anyone else winning the favor of the Angel of Death. In rage she shouted, "You undeserving sinners, let go of my feet! How dare you soar toward heaven with my charmed carrot?"

Kicking off the other sinners, she released her hold on the carrot. Thus, she and the whole chain plunged down through space, dropping with a thud on the floor of Hades.

The moral of the story is that even a small act of goodness may be a tiny raft of salvation across the treacherous gulf of sin, but one who drinks the wine of selfishness, and dances on the little boat of meanness, sinks in the ocean of ignorance. Selfish happiness, which cannot bear to witness the well being of others, is bound to come to grief.

My Pet Deer

In God there is no separation, but for those who have not realized the oneness of God, there is separation and death. They see death as a blank wall where souls are gone and forgotten. The person of realization sees beyond the land of death, where all souls are dancing and awakening again. Death should not cause sorrow. How sad I used to feel when friends passed away. You must not feel this way. When you know God, you will see everyone in the great Divine; then you will realize that they are never really away from you.

Once, in India at our school in Ranchi, I became very fond of a little deer. I loved the fawn so much that I allowed it to sleep in my room. At the light of dawn, the little creature would toddle over to my bed for a morning caress.

One day I was going away from the school. Although I cautioned the boys not to feed the fawn until my return, one of them gave the baby deer a large quantity of milk. When I came back in the evening, sad news greeted me: "The little fawn is nearly dead, through overfeeding." I almost died with sorrow. I said, "If there is a God, He will not take my deer away." So I began to meditate, and after three hours the deer got up. God had given him back to me.

But what a lesson I learned later! I stayed up with the fawn until two a.m. when I fell asleep. The deer appeared in a dream, and spoke to me:

"You are holding me back. Please let me go; let me go!"

"All right," I answered in the dream.

I awoke immediately, and cried out, "Boys, the deer is dying!" The children rushed to my side.

I ran to the corner of the room where I had placed the pet. It made a last effort to rise, stumbled toward me, then dropped at my feet, dead.

According to the mass karma that guides and regulates the destinies of animals, the deer's life was over, and it was ready to progress to a higher form. But by my deep attachment, which I later realized was selfish, and by my fervent prayers, I had been able to hold it in the limitations of the animal form from which the soul was struggling for release. The soul of the deer made its plea in a dream because, without my loving permission, it either would not or could not go. A soon as I agreed, it departed.

All sorrow left me; I realized anew that God wants His children to love everything as a part of Him, and not to feel delusively that death ends all. The ignorant man sees only the insurmountable wall of death, hiding, seemingly forever, his cherished friends. But the man of nonattachment, he who loves others as expressions of the Lord, understands that at death the dear ones have only returned for a breathing space of joy in Him.

The Last Day

You who are reading, and I who am writing, and all the two billion people throbbing with life today* will exist a hundred years hence only as thoughts. Great and small must be buried beneath the grass or thrown into the flames of cremation. We, who are so sure of our breakfasts, lunches, and dinners, will be unable to swallow or to speak. Our lips will be sealed forever.

We who love to listen to flattery, to the voice of the brook, to the sweet melody of music, and to the familiar words of our loved ones, must one day never again hear any sound from this sad earth.

The roses and blossoms that you love, some day will send the messenger of sweet fragrance to knock at the door of your perfume-loving sense, but the door of that sense will open no more. You will never again be lured by Nature's earthly perfume.

The day will arrive when all beautiful things will stand mutely at the wisdom gate of your lotus gaze and will try to get into the chamber of your appreciation, but you will behold imperfect matter no more.

*Written in 1934.

The chamber of wisdom will be left untenanted. The brain that controlled your 27 trillion cells and your bodily factory will direct them no more. The soft touches of the breeze and the warmth of the sunshine will soothe you no more, for your body will remain inert and lifeless.

The day will come when you cannot see, when you cannot move your hands or feet, and when you will have neither good nor bad thoughts, success nor failure, wisdom nor ignorance.

Since this must come to pass, why are you building the conviction of permanent comfort around this melting butter-doll of a body? The heat of death will melt these frozen bodily atoms. Did you ever think that you have only this one life, and that then you will join the shadows of millions of souls who have also thought, lived, laughed, and died with unfulfilled hopes?

Reincarnation is undoubtedly true, but do you realize that you will never have the same body, the same mind, friends in the same forms, or the same way to live and die as you will experience in this life?

Remember, you have to play one role for a few years of sorrow and laughter on the screen of time, then this particular film of life will be shelved forever, never to be played again, though revamped and played on the screen of some other incarnation.

If each and every soul's cheap garment of flesh must be discarded, that the soul may put on the shining robes of immortality, why should you cry? If both immortality-declaring saints and trembling-at-death small men must die, then why fear death? It is a universal experience through which all must pass.

Think what a mystery Life is! It has its origin in the unknown, and into the unknown it merges. Think what a mystery Death is! It swallows up the hard-working man and the idle man alike, and makes them change back into ether and the elements. Think how everybody fears death, and yet death comes only to give peace and relief, when life's burden grows too heavy with grief, ill health, or apparently incurable troubles.

Why spend all the treasure of your wisdom trying to make this uncertain, perishable body comfortable? Wake up! Try to reap the harvest of imperishable immortality and lasting, ever-new bliss on the perishable soil of the body. You will never find lasting comfort from a slowly dissolving body. You can never squeeze the honey of divine happiness from the rock of sense pleasures.

Lasting comfort flows ceaselessly into the pail of your life when you squeeze the honeycomb of meditation and peace with the eager, powerful hands of will, and with ever-deeper concentration.

Why intoxicate yourself with material desires during your death-like sleep of ignorance? Your present material activity is like walking in a dream of delusion during the sleep of ignorance. Why are you so sure of yourself, and why do you devote your entire time to building a material fortune that you must leave behind you in an instant at the call of death? As you know, material riches are too heavy to be carried in your astral car when you journey to the great Beyond. Why not prepare now for the last day on earth, when you will have to leave behind you everything to which you are so attached?

I do not mean that you should be a cynic and not enjoy the things of this life. All I say is, do not be so attached to anything that you will feel mental agony when you forcibly lose it or are separated from it. If you do not grieve for earthly things when your bodily garment is cast off, you will have better things hereafter. You will again receive from the hands of your Father, God, all the things that you ever cherished and lost. He takes things from you so that you will not remain earthbound and forgetful of your true immortal state.

Acquire the power of meditation and the treasures of intuitional perceptions and ever-new peace and joy, which will be of greater use to you on your last journey. Forget the delusions of today. Get ready for death, by making your acquaintance with God every day. At the end of the trail, through the portals of that last day, you will be allowed entry into the Kingdom of your Father, and remain there forever.

Spiritual Resurrection

Life is glorious; life is beautiful, if you will only find God beneath the debris of matter. You must not be hypnotized by this changing picture of life and death, but behold immortality. It is the most joyous thing that you can experience. God is hidden behind the moon and the sun and the stars. Your very conscience is the voice of God. And there is no other way to uncover God except by real devotion and meditation.

Every day, resurrect yourself in meditation. Compare your state before and after meditation. Meditate deeply if you would know God. Let your evil habits, indifference, and restlessness die daily.

Resurrection means relaxation, to relax your awareness from your body and mind in meditation. Then you become free: your soul knows that you can live without the body though still living in the body; it is separate.

Human life may be beautiful, but it is like a bird's life in a cage. You open the cage door, but the bird does not want to fly away. It is afraid—and we, also, in meditation, say, "Will I slip into the Infinite and never come back?" We are afraid of the vast sky. We have lived identified too long with the body, and are afraid of our own infinite omnipresence, afraid to resurrect our omnipotence, our omniscience.

You do not know what joy lies beyond the screen of the subconscious mind. If you do away with the restlessness and sensations of the body, sit quietly, and say: "In the Heaven of Silence, O God, be born within me," then on the altar of silence He will come. The joy of God is indescribable—joy that no changing dream of life and death can ever take away from you.

Chapter 5

Reincarnation

The Theory of Reincarnation

There has been a great deal of controversy as to whether reincarnation is true. If there is no truth in the theory of reincarnation, it is useless to believe in any form of religion. Reincarnation teaches that life continues after so-called death. The body does not last, but the soul lasts forever—the permanent soul in a temporary body. The soul cannot go back to God until it reaches perfection. Hence, when the body perishes, the soul must have another body in order to overcome its imperfections.

The body is the residence and the soul is the resident. The fleshly house is perishable and the soul, being the image of Spirit, is imperishable. Therefore, when the body dies, the soul has to shift somewhere else for shelter. Because of the soul's intimate contact with the body, it develops physical desires. These imperfect material attachments cling to the disembodied soul and prevent it from returning to the Spirit. Thus, the immortal soul has no other alternative but to come back to the mortal school of life, where alone it can work out its imperfections.

When a child is sent to school and fails to make the grade, he has to go back again and again until he passes his examinations. So also, souls who fail to preserve their perfection while in the mortal school of education and entertainment have to come back for many incarnations, until they experience completely their hidden Spirit nature. The immortal soul must win several prizes in order to maintain Spirit-endurance: self-control, detachment, morality, calmness, and spirituality—and must pass all grades in the earthly school in order to become free.

Immortal soul children are sent to the movie house of Life to make or to watch pictures of Life, both tragedies and comedies, with an unruffled equanimity. When these divine children can go back to God and say, "Father, I enjoyed acting in and watching Thy earthly moving pictures, but I have no more desire for evanescent amusements," they are no longer forced by their material desires to come back to earth.

God sent perfect souls to earth to behave like immortals—calm, desireless, and ever happy—both to watch the earthly moving pictures and to act in them. During the acting and watching of mundane moving pictures, however, souls develop attachments. Unless its material desires are cast off before death, the soul must return to another body in the earthly moving picture house in order to work out the desires born there.

If you die with the desire to possess a Rolls Royce, you won't be able to live forever in heaven where souls glide about without vehicles. You will therefore have to come back to earth, where alone that particular desire can be fulfilled. Even the highest outward desire on the part of the soul is limiting when compared to the eternal kingdom of the cosmos, which the soul loses owing to its concentration on little things.

How Reincarnation Can Be Prevented

If the perfect soul-children of God come on earth and do everything to please God rather than to satisfy the craving of their egos, then they will be free from the necessity for reincarnation. Therefore, whenever you eat (for example), think, "I eat not because of greed, but only to maintain Thy temple of consciousness, and to please Thee, since Thou has given me the urge of hunger." Or, think, "I earn money only to discharge my heaven-given responsibility to maintain myself and others, and not out of avarice." Whatever you are doing, tell yourself, "I think, I will, and I am happy to please Thee alone."

Working for God is very enjoyable and is also personally satisfying. Working for your own ego is personally blinding, and creates misery. Therefore, perform all good deeds not for yourself but for God. In this way, the responsibility for your actions and for their results will not touch the soul. This mental attitude cuts the cord of attachment that brings souls back to earth. When you eat, work, think, play, meditate, and enjoy true earthly happiness just to please God, and not to please yourself, you are ever ready to remain here or to leave the earth without sorrow or attachment, according to God's pleasure. Then you will not be forced back to earth.

Actions performed to please God leave no attachment. If you eat strawberry pie or make money with the consciousness of pleasing God, you do not carry the desire for those fulfillments with you when you die. If you act with greed or selfishness, and die with those desires unfulfilled, you will have to come back to earth to fulfill them. This does not mean you must be without ambition. The lazy or negligent person isn't ambitious to please God by good actions on earth, so he must come back here until he learns to work energetically with the one purpose of pleasing God.

The egotist, who works only to please himself, becomes caught in an endless net of desires, from which he can extricate himself only after many incarnations. Therefore, never be idle, absent-minded, or egotistically ambitious, but be divinely ambitious to work and play on earth with the right attitude of mind, as the Divine Director wishes of you.

To leave the world and go to the forest to meditate is one extreme, but your earthly desires can follow you to the forest. To be merged in the world, but not *of* the world, or better still, to enjoy the world with the pure joy of God, brings lasting happiness.

To renounce the world without the inner conquest of desires produces hypocrites. To be in the world without spiritual training makes you hard and worldly. To do everything in the world to please God is the highest ideal, according to the Hindu scripture the Bhagavad Gita, the lofty teachings of which are compatible with both Western and Eastern life. If we live as hermits in the forests, we may not live hygienically, and may die from disease. If we live in the world without peace, we may die of mental worry. Keep God in your heart, therefore, wherever you are, smile with His joy, and work for Truth alone.

Why Reincarnation Is To Be Avoided

As immortal soul-children of God, we must not be forced by the fruits of our own evil actions to return to undesirable lives on earth. Our home is in omnipresence: the diseaseless, sorrowless, ever-blessed kingdom of God. It is not this caravanserai of earth, where we descend for earthly entertainment. When we are through with this mundane play, we must make up our minds to return home.

Reincarnation is created by the satanic force, which has instilled in people wrong desires and attachments, and has influenced them to leave the all-happy kingdom of God and to return repeatedly to earth, the land of false hopes, disillusionment, bereavement, and ignorance.

The Ego Loves the Bodily Jail

Reincarnation keeps immortal souls away from their kingdom of omnipresence in the disease-ridden, accident-prone, and misery-infested little bodily jail. Just as some criminals get so used to jail that they hate to leave it at the end of their term, so also omnipresent souls become so attached that they hate to leave the bodily jail, even when their life term expires.

Free souls like Jesus, Krishna, and our great Guru Babaji, can visit the earthly prison to bring parole for soul prisoners, recalling them to their kingdom of unending happiness.

Authority for Reincarnation

Two hundred million Hindus, five hundred million Chinese, millions of Japanese,* and a host of other nationalities believe in reincarnation. Pythagoras, the eminent poet Emerson, businessmen like Henry Ford, and world-famous scientists like Thomas Edison and Luther Burbank all believed in reincarnation. The Hindu Masters, and Jesus also, knew of and endorsed the doctrine of reincarnation.

Jesus said, "But I say unto you, that Elias is come already, and they knew him not . . ." "Then the disciples understood that He spake unto them of John the Baptist." (Matthew 17:12-13)

In the words of Jesus, we find clearly enunciated the law of reincarnation. The prophet Elias was a soul in a body. When his body died, his soul passed into heaven and returned to earth for further incarnations, then slipped into the body

* Written in 1934.

of John the Baptist. What else could this quotation mean than that the prophet Elias was reborn as John the Baptist?

In Revelation, Chapter 3:12, we read: "Him that overcometh will I make a pillar in the temple of my God, and he shall go no more out." He that overcomes his bodily desires will become a fixed soul (pillar) in the mansion of God's presence, and he will not have to go again to the earth in pursuit of earthly fulfillments.

Revelation, Chapter 2:7, states: "To him that overcometh will I give to eat of the tree of life, which is in the midst of the paradise of God." He that overcomes the desires of the body will not come to earth to taste the bittersweet fruits of earthly life, but will enjoy God, or the "tree of life," which is ever-present in the paradise of ever-living, divine happiness.

The highest Hindu scripture, the Bhagavad Gita, says: "I, the supreme Spirit, reincarnate myself again and again in order to uplift the oppressors and redeem the virtuous."

As a man, forsaking one worn-out garment, puts on a new one, so also, the soul, leaving a tattered body, betakes itself to a new fleshly dwelling.

Isaac Newton, Galileo, and Jules Verne predicted many truths, which they foresaw. Galileo was punished for knowing and teaching that the Earth is round, when all the people on the globe at that time thought it was flat.

Thus Jesus and other wise men have realized the truth about reincarnation. When people do not understand a truth, they have to rely on the authoritative teaching of divine "super-sons," such as Jesus.

What Reincarnates?

The physical body contains, hidden, two other bodies, the astral body and the spiritual (idea) body.

If a pint of salt water is put in a jar and corked, and this then is placed into another larger jar and corked, and these two jars are put finally into a third, larger jar and corked, and the three jars are then placed in the ocean, the salt water in the inner jars cannot mingle with the sea water when the outermost jar is broken. All the three imprisoning jars must be broken to allow the water to merge into the ocean. Likewise, the physical body has the astral body and the ideational body, or causal, body within it; the soul is encased finally, within the idea body and corked with ignorance.

Thus, when the physical body is destroyed at death, the soul is not yet free. It can only find soul-freedom when the corks of ignorance from the astral and idea bodies are removed also, enabling it to mingle with the ocean of Spirit. As we put on three sets of clothing—an undergarment, a suit, and an overcoat—so the soul at death loses only the overcoat of the physical body.

The Three Bodies

The physical body is composed of sixteen gross metallic and nonmetallic elements: iron, phosphorus, chlorine, sodium, iodine, potassium, and so forth.

The astral body is composed of mental, emotional, and lifetronic elements, including: intelligence; ego; feeling; mind (sense-consciousness); five instruments of *knowledge*, the subtle counterparts of the senses of sight, hearing, smell, taste, touch; five instruments of *action*, the mental correspondence for the abilities to procreate, excrete, talk, walk, and exercise manual skill; and five instruments of *life force*, which perform the crystallizing, assimilating, eliminating, metabolizing, and circulating functions of the body.

If the crystallizing current in the body refuses to function properly, for example, tuberculosis starts. If the circulating current works irregularly, an anemic condition prevails.

The idea body consists of the seed ideas corresponding to the sixteen elements of the physical body and the nineteen elements of the astral body. God had to create all the elements in the physical and astral bodies as ideas first. These thought-created physical and astral elements were then vibrated grossly into physical and astral elements. Before God created iron, or thought, or feeling, for example, He had to create them in His mind first. In a dream, the difference between a dream-materialized rock and a flash of thought consists only in different kinds of ideas.

The physical body is destroyed at death, yet it is created again by earthly desires. Consciousness directs all material creation.

How to Release the Soul from Its Three Bodies

First, destroy earthly desires; then, by higher meditation learn to take your soul out of the bondage of the three bodies into the ocean of Spirit. If you can do that with the help of a true guru while you are physically alive, you will be able to do so when your physical body dies.

Reasons for Reincarnation

If you transgress the laws of health by over-eating, it is quite likely that you will be born with indigestion or tendencies toward stomach trouble, which result in an early death. After you pay the karma of overeating in the next incarnation, in the third one you may be born with the tendency to overeat, but may also live long enough to overcome greed, if that is your choice.

Babies who die in their mother's womb are usually suicide cases from before. They spurned life before, and in the process of re-birth they emanate spasms of latent repulsions of life, which derange the body so much that it dies in the embryo. Those who had acquired riches, health, prosperity, wisdom, or spirituality in past lives are born with specific advantages from the beginning of their present lives. Likewise, those who created poverty, disease, and ignorance through negligence in past lives will meet those conditions from the very beginning of their present lives.

This law of action, which dictates that you reap in this life what you sowed in a past life, is a just and wise law. It releases God from the man-imposed stigma of being an autocrat, who creates some brains healthy and some brains idiotic just for variety. This law of action explains the apparent injustices from the very beginning of human life. It also gives hope to all, for the sinner is a sinner not because his parents gave him sinful tendencies, but because he was sinful in a past life and thus attracted sinful parents.

Medical doctors would say that John inherited insanity from his insane father, but the metaphysician would say that John attracted an insane parent in this life because his soul brought back the tendency of insanity from his former life. This latter doctrine alone gives faith in the justice and wisdom of the working of God's laws in the lives of men.

If a person lives one hundred years, he has time to struggle against evil and to become good, but if a child dies at the age of five he does not have time to use his reason and free choice to win the battle of life. Such a young child dies because of some former, self-inflicted transgression. He must be born again and again in various schools of life until he educates himself to right behavior.

If babies go to heaven when they die, why not drown all the babies at birth, and save having to face the struggle of existence? When a bandit dies, he does not become an angel by the mere virtue of death. Those who live desultory lives, and yet expect to become angels after death, will be disappointed. We are the same after a night's sleep as before it. Sinful or virtuous souls are respectively the same after physical death.

As souls, we are already rays of God's light. We can remain hidden behind clouds of sin, just as the sun hides for a while behind a cloud, but we cannot hide the soul forever. Not all the sins of the cosmos could destroy our essential luminosity; we must remove the choking clouds of ignorance and re-manifest our everlasting light.

We must not reason that since we will someday be redeemed, let us tarry on the way. That is foolish, for sin is very painful. Why willingly suffer for eons of time, out of ignorance?

Why Ignorance of Former Lives Is No Proof Against Reincarnation

Memory is no test of pre-existence. We do not remember the nine months of our existence as embryos, nor do we remember when we were still babies. How, then, could we remember when we lived in a different body with a different brain and nervous system, and with a different appearance?

It is well that we do not remember the hard experiences in the school of past lives, for we would not like to be hypnotized once again with those hardships. If we remembered all the hard knocks we endured in our former lives, we might feel disinclined to be good again, or merely bored by the repetition, or helpless to reform if we wanted to. If we remembered our childhood days, our youth, and our old age, we would not like to live over again the wily pranks of childhood, the comedies of youth, and the tragedies of old age.

Think what a blessing reincarnation is! It smashes our old rickety car of life and gives us a brand new model in which to try at last to win the race of life!

All criminals, murderers, and men of lost reputation, shunned as they've been on earth, can come back to earth in new forms, ready to begin life anew, welcomed and encouraged by new friends in new circumstances.

Indications of Reincarnation

Certain Occidental people, Americans especially, are like the most spiritual Hindus, and certain Hindus act like hard-boiled American businessmen. Many spiritual Hindus have taken American bodies in order, in the divine plan, to spiritualize America. Likewise, many Americans who loved the materially downfallen but spiritually great Hindus have taken birth in India in order to free her.

Think as far back as you can remember, then enumerate your first unalloyed tendencies. Did you love incense or oriental philosophy, or did you love tools and machinery? Those early tendencies, separated from the acquired tendencies of this life, help to reveal your past.

Sometimes you find a family in which the members are constantly fighting; they were enemies in the past, and established hatred for one another in their hearts. Because the law of attraction involves hatred as well as love, nature has brought those enemy souls together again to continue the "fuss" of fighting each other within the narrow arena of a small home. Beware, therefore! Do not attract your enemy, nor his bad qualities, by concentrating on him constantly through the hatred you feel for him.

A Long Process

Reincarnation begins at the crystals stage. It reaches the human level of existence after eight million lives. How very long it takes for the soul to evolve to birth in the body of a man. Matter suppresses the Spirit, which seeks ever to reform matter from within, by coaxing its evolution.

Metals, vegetables, and human beings: the bodies are different, but the soul is ever the same. Reincarnation is the process through which the Spirit returns to Itself—from the many to the one.

The Origin of Reincarnation

God made man immortal. The plan was for him to remain on earth as an immortal. He was to behold the drama of change with a changeless immortal consciousness and, after seeing the dance of change on the stage of changelessness, he was to return to the bosom of eternal blessedness. Then evil crept in. It caused man to concentrate on life's changes, and on outward appearances rather than on the immortality underlying all things; with this came the false idea of death as complete annihilation.

Destroying the Idea of Death

The motion picture of a man's life—his birth, life on earth, and death—shows happiness in birth and sadness in death. Satanic ignorance, however, hides from man's view the motion pictures of his pre-existence, as he joyously descended from God, and his joyous return to higher realms after death. Satan has made us forget our prenatal and postnatal experiences by showing us all too briefly this drama of life, then lowering the curtain, producing in us thereby an erroneous concept of death.

To say that death or change does not exist is erroneous, but I consider death only an outward link in the chain of immortality, the rest of which is hidden from our view. To forget dismal, delusive death, man should behold all change as dancing on the bosom of changelessness.

Supernatural Death Versus Painful Death

If Adam and Eve had not transgressed the wishes of God, and their descendants had not allowed themselves to be influenced by hereditary ignorance, then modern man would not have had to witness heartrending painful deaths through accident and disease.

Man appeared on earth materialized by God, and was meant to live on earth enjoying birth, growth, and a painless return of the body to complete perfection. As it is possible to watch on the movie screen the slow process of a flower budding, growing, and disappearing, so man should behold his life pictured on the screen of his consciousness through the stages from childhood to adulthood, and then his disappearance in God of his own accord by his own power of dematerialization.

Man, being out of tune with God, has lost his power of dematerialization. He is therefore frightened by the moving picture of life, and the threat of being cut off prematurely. This premature withdrawal of the motion picture of life produces pain owing to attachment to those movie images of flesh and consciousness. That withdrawal is known by worldly people as terrible death.

We mortals have so many misconceptions about death that it has gained importance in our minds as an idea of annihilation and pain, instead of being seen as a necessary phenomenon for the soul to return from the state of change to the changeless state.

How Reincarnation Was Created by Satan

Satan saw that if the immortal children of God lived a perfect earthly existence, with a changeless attitude, they would quickly return to the state of immortality. Satan's earthly dominion would cease to exist. He therefore tampered with life's perfect picture, and, through delusion, caused mental and bodily pain. The ensuing pains of life caused dissatisfaction, creating in man the desire to experience life without pain.

The immortal children of God forgot their awareness of their perfect immortality and, instead, desired mortal, delusive perfection. Their desires for human satisfaction caused them to reincarnate again and again, according to the law of cause and effect which governs desires. This law, the law of Karma (action), has kept souls imprisoned on earth in Satan's kingdom of finitude.

How to Destroy Reincarnation

Immortal souls can only expect to find freedom by utterly destroying all seeds of earthly desires, through contact with God in meditation. Meditation reminds the soul of the unending fulfillment in the immortal inheritance of bliss, and makes all desires for earthly ways unnecessary and, indeed, ridiculous.

Knowledge of Wholeness

Emancipation from reincarnation is possible also by playing the drama of a perfect life of health, abundance, and wisdom on the screen of consciousness. For example, if we can remove the consciousness of sickness and not fear sickness if it does come, nor desire health when we suffer from ill health, then we can remember the soul, which is forever well. Equanimity, in other words, is a secret to freedom from the need to reincarnate. If we can feel and know that, as children of God, we possess everything even as our Father does, whether we are outwardly poor or rich, we can achieve freedom. If we can feel that we have divine knowledge because we are made in the image of God, although humanly speaking we know little—then we can free ourselves from reincarnation.

Fear of sickness, and a desire for physical health, fear of poverty, and a desire for opulence, and the feeling that we lack knowledge as well as the desire to know everything: all these belong in the domain of ignorance. Of course, if we are stricken with ill health, failure, or ignorance, we need not continue to remain so. We should strive for health, prosperity, and wisdom without fear of failure. But we should remain non-attached and even-minded, throughout.

Know That Imperfections Are Delusions

While struggling, man must know that his struggle for health, prosperity, and wisdom is born of delusion, for he already has all he needs within his inner all-powerful Self. It is the erroneous thought that he does not have these things that is the source of his sense of lack. He needs only to know that he has everything already.

Once a healthy, wealthy, and wise prince dreamed that he was poor. In the dream he shouted, "Oh, I am suffering from cancer and I have lost all my wisdom and riches." His wife, the queen, woke up and roused him, saying, "Look, prince, laugh and rejoice, for you are neither suffering from sickness nor have you lost your riches and wisdom. You are lying comfortably at my side with health and wisdom, in your rich kingdom. You were only dreaming these catastrophes."

So it is with ignorant man. He is dreaming lack and failure, when he can claim his birthright of joy, health, and plenty as a son of the Ruler of the universe. He is now living in God's perfect kingdom, but he is dreaming imperfection.

Know God First

The constant desire for health and prosperity, which is so much harped upon in modern spiritual organizations, is the way to slavery. We must seek God first, and find our health and prosperity in Him. Beggars get only a beggar's pittance, whereas a son of God gets a son's inheritance. That is why Jesus said we should seek first the kingdom of God. When that is accomplished, health and prosperity will be added. The acquirement of wisdom and everything else that the soul of man needs will be received as his divine birthright.

It is best to feel, by visualization and by divine contact in meditation, that you are already in perfect health, wisdom and abundance, rather than trying to succeed by begging for health, prosperity, and wisdom. In fact, man's mortal efforts are bound by the laws of cause and effect. Man cannot get more than he deserves. No human being can ever fulfill his endless desires by begging; but by first realizing his oneness with God, man can own everything he needs.

Man cannot have immortality by merely desiring it, or begging for it. He should know that he is already immortal, and that so-called death is only a dream.

According to the plan of God, man should have experienced growth from childhood through youth to manhood, but should never have experienced death by old age or disease. Even when man becomes old, he should never die of disease or suffer painful death. In the drama of life and death, when beheld with divine understanding, there is only the showing or stopping at will of the motion picture of life, without physical or mental pain.

The Origin of Pain

The outward flowing force which struggles to keep all things in manifestation (Satan) saw that, without pain, people would not create earthly desires to hold them here, so he created the illusion of pain, which is a purely a mental phenomenon.

But Satan is defeating his own purpose, for it is physical pain and sorrow that cause matter-imprisoned souls to seek freedom in God. A child's pure soul feels very little pain. A doctor friend in an orthopedic hospital told me that children vie with each other to get their deformed limbs operated upon, whereas adults have to be coaxed for weeks, and at the time of surgery they are usually overcome with emotion and fear.

Man, fortunately, has discovered anesthetics to neutralize pain. Originally, man had great self-control and a mind which was unattached and impersonal, and so he did not feel pain when the body was injured. He could behold his own body without pain, even as one can witness an operation on another person's body without becoming mentally excited or suffering physical pain.

If you have no fear or nervous imagination, you will feel less pain. The farmer's waterproof, heatproof, and less sensitive child feels much less physical suffering than the sensitively brought up son of the rich man.

Satan Is a Part of God's Drama

There cannot be two absolute causes in the universe. Satan is a part of God's drama. He is necessary to it, as the villain is necessary in a stage play. Evil is the veil that conceals God, the magnet that tries to draw the mind away from Him. Good is that which helps to make God's hidden reality manifest, like the breeze, blowing away the smoke hiding a fire.

Within the realm of duality, however, both good and evil exist. God, the Supreme Spirit, is beyond them both. Being omniscient, He knows them both equally—the evil as much as the good. Goodness, however, reveals more clearly to the mind the existence of bliss, which, since it is above relativity, may be described as goodness absolute. The satanic force, on the other hand, being conscious, tries deliberately to hide from man's gaze that ever-blazing light of divinity.

REINCARNATION IN A NUTSHELL

There was a man who loved God and had achieved a little spiritual advancement, but who also had a few worldly desires left to fulfill. At the end of his life an angel appeared to him and asked, "Is there anything you still want?"

"Yes," the man said, "All my life I've been weak, thin, and unwell. I would like in my next life to have a strong, healthy body."

In his next life he was given a strong, large, and healthy body. He was poor, however, and found it difficult to keep that robust body properly fed. At last—still hungry—he lay dying. The angel appeared to him again and asked, "Is there anything more you desire?"

"Yes," he replied. "For my next life, I would like a strong, healthy body, and also a healthy bank account!"

Well, the next time he had a strong, healthy body, and was also wealthy. In time, however, he began to grieve that he had no one with whom to share his good fortune. When death came, the angel asked, "Is there anything else?"

"Yes, please. Next time, I would like to be strong, healthy, and wealthy, and also to have a good woman for a wife."

Well, in his next life he was given all those blessings. His wife, too, was a good woman. Unfortunately, she died in her youth. For the rest of his days, he grieved at that loss. He worshiped her gloves, her shoes, and other memorabilia that were precious to him. As he lay dying of grief, the angel appeared to him again and said, "What now?"

"Next time," said the man, "I would like to be strong, healthy, and wealthy, and also to have a good wife who lives a long time."

"Are you sure you've covered everything?" demanded the angel.

"Yes, I'm certain that's everything this time."

Well, in his next life he had all those things, including a good wife who lived a long time. The trouble was, she lived too long! As he grew older, he became infatuated with his beautiful young secretary, to the point where, finally, he left his good wife for that girl. As for the girl, all she wanted was his money. When she'd got her hands on it, she ran away with a much younger man. At last, as the man lay dying, the angel again appeared to him and demanded. "Well, what is it this time?"

"Nothing!" the man cried. "Nothing ever again! I've learned my lesson. I see that, in every fulfillment, there is always a catch. From now on, whether I'm rich or poor, healthy or unhealthy, married or single, whether here on this earth or in the astral plane, I want only my divine Beloved. Wherever God is, there alone lies perfection!"

Reincarnation Scientifically Proved

If one believes in the existence of a just God, then a belief in reincarnation can follow very readily, as the two beliefs are really dependent on one another. But what about the skeptics and the atheists? Can the truth of reincarnation be scientifically proven to their satisfaction?

Material scientists claim that they have not found any actual proof of the existence of a God, and hence cannot offer any proof of the existence of His just law, which gives equal opportunity to all life to improve through reincarnation. To such scientists, the sufferings of innocent babies, and the other inequalities of life, seem inexplicable and point to the absence of any just God.

Scientific Law

On the other hand, most of those who do believe in a just God base their faith on belief only and have no scientific proof to offer the unbelievers. For the most part, they do not dare to scrutinize or deeply question their faith, for fear of losing it or of creating social disharmony. They are not aware, in other words, of the existence of a scientific spiritual law that can prove their beliefs to be truth.

Why shouldn't the methods of experimentation used by scientists to discover physical truths be applied to investigating spiritual law? This question was asked centuries ago by the Hindu savants, and they set about the task of answering it. Their experiments resulted in scientific methods which can be followed by anyone to discover the reality of spiritual law, and hence of reincarnation and many of the other great cosmic truths.

Since this method does exist, no one has the right to say that reincarnation and other spiritual laws do not operate until he has tried the method and seen the result for himself. A scientist is privileged to express his opinion, but it remains an opinion only and not a fact.

In physical science, certain methods must be adopted and followed in order to prove the truth of any given theory. To the naked eye, certain germs are not visible. One must use a microscope to detect the presence of the germs. If a person refuses to look through the microscope, he cannot be said to have scientifically tested the theory that germs were present. His opinion is therefore valueless, since he did not follow the prescribed rules for arriving at the truth of the theory. So it is in spiritual things. The method has been discovered, the rules laid down, and the result is open to anyone who is interested enough to experiment.

In the Western world, due to the lack of this scientific approach to spiritual law, the value of religion has greatly diminished as a living factor in the life of man; spiritual doctrines are believed in or rejected simply on the ground of personal bias rather than as a result of scientific investigation.

Experiments on the Consciousness of Man

The Master Minds of ancient India discovered unalterable cosmic laws through experiments on the life and thought of man, in the laboratories of their hermitages. To find the truth of physical things, we must experiment upon physical substances. To find the truth of reincarnation, or the passage of one soul through many bodies, it is necessary to experiment upon the consciousness of man.

Those ancient scientists found that the human ego (the soul identified with the body) outlasts all the changes of experience and thought during the states of wakefulness, dreaming, and deep sleep during one lifetime. Experiences change, the environment, sensations, thoughts, and bodily states change, but the sense of identity, of "I," does not change from birth to death. Hence, the Hindu experimenters argued that concentrating on the ego, through constant, conscious introspection or observation of the various changing states of life—of wakefulness, dream, or deep sleep—one could perceive the changeless and eternal nature of the ego.

Ordinarily one is conscious of his waking state, and, sometimes, of his dreaming state. Often people are aware that they are dreaming; even in their dream, they know that they are dreaming. So, through certain methods and practices, one can come to be aware of every state: of sleep, dream, and dreamless "deep sleep."

Relaxation in Sleep

During sleep, there is involuntary relaxation of energy from the motor and sensory nerves. Through yogic meditation practices, one can produce this relaxation during the waking state also, and at will. In the "big sleep" of death, there is still further relaxation—the retirement of energy from the heart and cerebro-spinal axis. But by certain yogic practices, this further relaxation may be produced consciously in the waking state. In other words, every involuntary function may be accomplished voluntarily and consciously by practice.

Ancient Hindus found that death was the withdrawal of the electricity of life from the bulb of human flesh, containing the wires of sensory and motor nerves to the different channels of outward expression. Just as electricity does not die when it is withdrawn from a broken bulb, so life energy is not annihilated when it retires from the involuntary nerves. It withdraws at death, to the Cosmic Energy.

Current Withdrawn

In sleep, the conscious mind ceases to operate—the current is temporarily withdrawn from the nerves; in death, the human consciousness ceases to express permanently through the body. It is as though one had a paralyzed arm—one is mentally conscious of that arm, but cannot function through it.

Medical records tell the case of a clergyman who once fell into a state of coma (suspended animation). He heard everyone around bewailing his apparent death, but he could not express his awareness through his physical organs. His body motor had "stalled" and refused to respond to his mental commands. At last, when his friends were about to take him to be embalmed, he made a supreme effort and was able to move, after twenty-four hours of apparent death. This instance illustrates the constancy of the awareness of "I-ness," or personal identity, even though the body is seemingly dead.

The Hindu teachers stated that one must learn to separate the energy and consciousness from the body, consciously. One must consciously watch the state of sleep and must practice the voluntary withdrawal of energy consciously from the heart and spinal regions. Thus he learns to do consciously what death will otherwise force upon him unconsciously and unwillingly.

An Amazing Case

There is a case in the files of European doctors of a man named Sadhu Haridas, who was able to separate his energy and consciousness from his body and then connect the two together again after several months. His body was buried underground, and the area was carefully watched day and night, for months. At the end of this time, his body was dug up and examined by the European doctors, who pronounced him dead. After a few minutes Sadhu Haridas opened his eyes, regained control over all the functions of his body, and lived for many more years. He had simply learned, by practice, how to control all the involuntary functions of his body and mind. He was a spiritual scientist who experimented with prescribed methods for learning the truth of cosmic law. As a result, he was in a position to demonstrate the truth of the theory of the changelessness of personal identity, and the eternal nature of the life principle.

Those who would know the scientific truth of the doctrine of reincarnation must follow the rules laid down many centuries ago by Hindu savants and must learn to disconnect themselves consciously, not passively as during sleep, from the five senses; and they must learn to control the action of the heart, that is, experience conscious death, or suspended animation. This is the art of separating the soul from the body.

Follow the Practices

By following practices that lead to the above results, we can follow the ego through all states of existence. We can follow it consciously through death, through space, to other bodies or other worlds. Those who do not learn these things cannot retain their sense of personal identity, of awareness or consciousness, during the big sleep of death, and hence cannot remember any previous state, or even the deep sleep states during one life.

By adopting the methods of the ancient Hindu scientists who experimented with such laws and who thereby gave the world a knowledge that is priceless and demonstrable, one may come to know the scientific truth of reincarnation and all other eternal verities.

The Way to Freedom

Only advanced souls who can live without breath or heartbeat can consciously experience the state of death, in which the breath and heart stop. Ordinary souls become unconscious when they stop breathing. Advanced souls can consciously go to the astral world, which follows after earthly death. So, practicing breathless silence is almost a condition, a passport, required to enter the spirit world consciously.

The problem of reincarnation is the greatest mystery, as nature does not want to discourage undeveloped souls. Supermen remember their past. I knew from my childhood that I was to follow the spiritual path and that galaxies of souls were to enliven my life.

Reincarnation requires souls to travel through the mineral, plant, animal, and human kingdoms, including all the races of brown, white, black, yellow, and red, so that they may transcend confinement to one body or one race, and may learn to perceive themselves as omnipresent children of God, present in everything.

As long as one has hatred and repulsion in his heart, so long must he keep roaming through the corridors of incarnations. After eight million lives, human life, according to Hindu masters, is finally attained. Do not waste this precious, hard-earned human life in foolishness, wading in the mud of the senses and ignorance, but realize that in this human life you have the chance, by conscious unity with omnipresent Spirit and by feeling brotherhood with all creatures, to know yourself as not wholly belonging to anything, or to any race, but as belonging to everything, and to every being.

When you feel that the stars, clouds, birds, beasts, men, and outcasts are all your blood relatives, and when your heart throbs in them, then you will no longer be compelled to reincarnate. You will freely go everywhere to open the rainbow gates of wisdom, so that all sorrowing animate and inanimate life may make a rushing exodus into the everlasting freedom in God.

Freedom from Reincarnation

The Bhagavad Gita describes reincarnation as a wheel, constantly turning. To get off the wheel, you have to desire freedom very intensely. Then only will God release you. Your longing has to be fervent. If it is, and if you are determined no more to want to play, the Lord has to release you. He tries to keep you here with tests, but in His higher aspect, as the Cosmic Lover, He hates this show, and wants you out of it. Why shouldn't He release you, once He sees that you really want Him alone, and not His show: that you want only freedom in Him?

The same essence—conscious life—is in you and in the tree. The tree, however, was put there, whereas some free will on your part made you who and what you are. Only the wise know just where predestination ends and free will begins. Meanwhile, you must keep on doing your best, according to your own clearest understanding. You must long for freedom as the drowning man longs for air. Without sincere longing, you will never find God. Desire Him above everything else. Desire Him that you may share Him with all: That is the greatest wish.

And try, meanwhile, to rise above the pairs of opposites: pleasure and pain, heat and cold, sickness and health. Free yourself from the consciousness of individuality, of being separate from everyone and everything else. Keep your mind fixed steadfastly on Him. Remain inwardly as unaffected as the motionless Spirit you want to become. He alone is what you really are. His bliss alone is your true nature.

Index

About Paramhansa Yogananda

"As a bright light shining in the midst of darkness, so was Yogananda's presence in this world. Such a great soul comes on earth only rarely, when there is a real need among men."

—The Shankaracharya of Kanchipuram

Born in India in 1893, Paramhansa Yogananda was trained from his early years to bring India's ancient science of Self-realization to the West. In 1920 he moved to the United States to begin what was to develop into a worldwide work touching millions of lives. Americans were hungry for India's spiritual teachings, and for the liberating techniques of yoga.

In 1946 he published what has become a spiritual classic and one of the best-loved books of the twentieth century, *Autobiography of a Yogi*. In addition, Yogananda established headquarters for a worldwide work, wrote a number of books and study courses, gave lectures to thousands in most major cities across the United States, wrote music and poetry, and trained disciples. He was invited to the White House by Calvin Coolidge, and he initiated Mahatma Gandhi into Kriya Yoga, his most advanced meditation technique.

Yogananda's message to the West highlighted the unity of all religions, and the importance of love for God combined with scientific techniques of meditation.

Further Explorations

The original 1946 unedited edition of Yogananda's spiritual masterpiece

AUTOBIOGRAPHY OF A YOGI

Paramhansa Yogananda

Autobiography of a Yogi is one of the best-selling Eastern philosophy titles of all time, with millions of copies sold, named one of the best and most influential books of the twentieth century. This highly prized reprinting of the original 1946 edition is the only one available free from textual changes made after Yogananda's death. Yogananda was the first yoga master of India whose mission was to live and teach in the West.

In this updated edition are bonus materials, including a last chapter that Yogananda wrote in 1951, without posthumous changes. This new edition also includes the eulogy that Yogananda wrote for Gandhi, and a new foreword and afterword by Swami Kriyananda, one of Yogananda's close, direct disciples.

Also available in unabridged audiobook (MP3) format, read by Swami Kriyananda.

PARAMHANSA YOGANANDA

A Biography with Personal Reflections and Reminiscences

Swami Kriyananda

Paramhansa Yogananda's classic *Autobiography of a Yogi* is more about the saints Yogananda met than about himself—in spite of Yogananda's astonishing accomplishments.

Now, one of Yogananda's direct disciples relates the untold story of this great spiritual master and world teacher: his teenage miracles, his challenges in coming to America, his national lecture campaigns, his struggles to fulfill his world-changing mission amid incomprehension and painful betrayals, and his ultimate triumphant achievement. Kriyananda's subtle grasp of his guru's inner nature reveals Yogananda's many-sided greatness. Includes many never-before-published anecdotes.

Also available in unabridged audiobook (MP3) format, read by Swami Kriyananda.

THE NEW PATH

My Life with Paramhansa Yogananda

Swami Kriyananda

When Swami Kriyananda discovered *Autobiography of a Yogi* in 1948, he was totally new to Eastern teachings. This is a great advantage to the Western reader, since Kriyananda walks us along the yogic path as he discovers it from the moment of his initiation as a disciple of Yogananda. With winning honesty, humor, and deep insight, he shares his journey on the spiritual path through personal stories and experiences.

Through more than four hundred stories of life with Yogananda, we tune in more deeply to this great master and to the teachings he brought to the West. This book is an ideal complement to *Autobiography of a Yogi.*

Also available in unabridged audiobook (MP3) format, read by Swami Kriyananda.

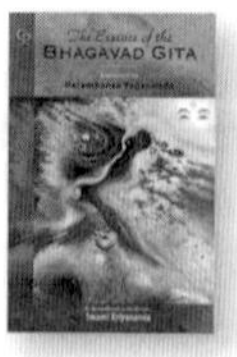

THE ESSENCE OF THE BHAGAVAD GITA

Explained by Paramhansa Yogananda

As Remembered by his disciple, Swami Kriyananda

Rarely in a lifetime does a new spiritual classic appear that has the power to change people's lives and transform future generations. This is such a book.

This revelation of India's best-loved scripture approaches it from a fresh perspective, showing its deep allegorical meaning and its down-to-earth practicality. The themes presented are universal: how to achieve victory in life in union with the divine; how to prepare for life's "final exam," death, and what happens afterward; and how to triumph over all pain and suffering.

Also available in unabridged audiobook (MP3) format, read by Swami Kriyananda.

DEMYSTIFYING PATANJALI: THE YOGA SUTRAS (APHORISMS)

The Wisdom of Paramhansa Yogananda

Presented by his direct disciple, Swami Kriyananda

A great spiritual master of ancient times—Patanjali—enlightened humanity through his *Yoga Sutras* with a step-by-step outline of how all spiritual aspirants achieve union with God. Since then, scholars have written commentaries that bury Patanjali's insights in confusing terms. Now, a modern yoga master—Paramhansa Yogananda—has resurrected Patanjali's original revelations. In *Demystifying Patanjali*, Swami Kriyananda shares Yogananda's crystal clear and easy-to-grasp explanations.

THE ESSENCE OF SELF-REALIZATION

The Wisdom of Paramhansa Yogananda

Recorded, Compiled, and Edited by his disciple, Swami Kriyananda

With nearly three hundred sayings rich with spiritual wisdom, this book is the fruit of a labor of love. A glance at the table of contents will convince the reader of the vast scope of this work. It offers as complete an explanation of life's true purpose, and of the way to achieve that purpose, as may be found anywhere.

Also available in unabridged audiobook (MP3) format, read by Swami Kriyananda.

CONVERSATIONS WITH YOGANANDA

Recorded, with Reflections, by his disciple, Swami Kriyananda

Here is an unparalleled, firsthand account of the teachings of Paramhansa Yogananda. Featuring nearly 500 never-before-released stories, sayings, and insights, this is an extensive, yet eminently accessible treasure trove of wisdom from one of the 20th century's most famous yoga masters. Compiled and edited with commentary by Swami Kriyananda, one of Yogananda's closest direct disciples.

REVELATIONS OF CHRIST

Proclaimed by Paramhansa Yogananda

Presented by his disciple, Swami Kriyananda

The rising tide of alternative beliefs proves that now, more than ever, people are yearning for a clear-minded and uplifting understanding of the life and teachings of Jesus Christ.

This galvanizing book, presenting the teachings of Christ from the exalted experience and perspective of Paramhansa Yogananda, one of the greatest spiritual masters of the twentieth century, finally offers the fresh perspective on Christ's teachings for which the world has been waiting. This book gives us an opportunity to understand and apply the scriptures in a more reliable way than any other: by studying under those saints who have communed directly, in deep ecstasy, with Christ and God.

Also available in unabridged audiobook (MP3) format, read by Swami Kriyananda.

WHISPERS FROM ETERNITY

Paramhansa Yogananda
Edited by his disciple, Swami Kriyananda

Many poetic works can inspire, but few, like this one, have the power to change your life. Yogananda was not only a spiritual master, but a master poet, whose verses revealed the hidden divine presence behind even everyday things. This book has the power to rapidly accelerate your spiritual growth, and provides hundreds of delightful ways for you to begin your own conversation with God.

Also available in unabridged audiobook (MP3) format, read by Swami Kriyananda.

THE RUBAIYAT OF OMAR KHAYYAM EXPLAINED

Paramhansa Yogananda
Edited by Swami Kriyananda

The *Rubaiyat* is loved by Westerners as a hymn of praise to sensual delights. In the East its quatrains are considered a deep allegory of the soul's romance with God, based solely on the author Omar Khayyam's reputation as a sage and mystic. But for centuries the meaning of this famous poem has remained a mystery. Now Paramhansa Yogananda reveals the secret import and the "golden spiritual treasures" hidden behind the *Rubaiyat's* verses—and presents a new scripture to the world.

~ THE WISDOM OF YOGANANDA SERIES ~

This series features writings of Paramhansa Yogananda not available elsewhere—including many from his earliest years in America—in an approachable, easy-to-read format. The words of the Master are presented with minimal editing, to capture his expansive and compassionate wisdom, his sense of fun, and his practical spiritual guidance.

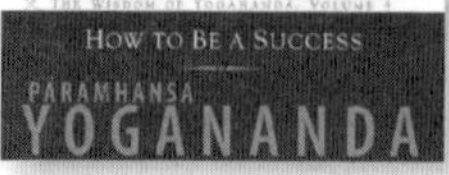

HOW TO BE HAPPY ALL THE TIME

The Wisdom of Yogananda Series, VOLUME **1,**
Paramhansa Yogananda

Yogananda powerfully explains virtually everything needed to lead a happier, more fulfilling life. Topics include: looking for happiness in the right places; choosing to be happy; tools and techniques for achieving happiness; sharing happiness with others; balancing success and happiness; and many more.

KARMA AND REINCARNATION

The Wisdom of Yogananda Series, VOLUME **2,**
Paramhansa Yogananda

Yogananda reveals the truth behind karma, death, reincarnation, and the afterlife. With clarity and simplicity, he makes the mysterious understandable. Topics include: why we see a world of suffering and inequality; how to handle the challenges in our lives; what happens at death, and after death; and the purpose of reincarnation.

SPIRITUAL RELATIONSHIPS

The Wisdom of Yogananda Series, VOLUME **3,**
Paramhansa Yogananda

This book contains practical guidance and fresh insights on relationships of all types. Topics include: how to cure bad habits that can end true friendship; how to choose the right partner; sex in marriage and how to conceive a spiritual child; problems that arise in marriage; and the Universal Love behind all your relationships.

HOW TO BE A SUCCESS

The Wisdom of Yogananda Series, VOLUME **4,**
Paramhansa Yogananda

This volume includes the complete text of *The Attributes of Success,* the original booklet later published as *The Law of Success.* In addition, you will learn how to find your purpose in life, develop habits of success and eradicate habits of failure, develop your will power and magnetism, and thrive in the right job.

HOW HAVE COURAGE, CALMNESS, AND CONFIDENCE

The Wisdom of Yogananda Series, VOLUME **5,**
Paramhansa Yogananda

This book shows you how to transform your life. Dislodge negative thoughts and depression. Uproot fear and thoughts of failure. Cure nervousness and systematically eliminate worry from your life. Overcome anger, sorrow, oversensitivity, and a host of other troublesome emotional responses; and much more.

HOW TO ACHIEVE GLOWING HEALTH AND VITALITY

The Wisdom of Yogananda Series, VOLUME **6,**
Paramhansa Yogananda

Paramhansa Yogananda, a foremost spiritual teacher of modern times, offers practical, wide-ranging, and fascinating suggestions on how to have more energy and live a radiantly healthy life. The principles in this book promote physical health and all-round well-being, mental clarity, and ease and inspiration in your spiritual life.

Readers will discover the priceless Energization Exercises for rejuvenating the body and mind, the fine art of conscious relaxation, and helpful diet tips for health and beauty.

THE ART AND SCIENCE OF RAJA YOGA

Swami Kriyananda

Contains fourteen lessons in which the original yoga science emerges in all its glory—a proven system for realizing one's spiritual destiny. This is the most comprehensive course available on yoga and meditation today. Over 450 pages of text and photos give you a complete and detailed presentation of yoga postures, yoga philosophy, affirmations, meditation instruction, and breathing practices.

Also included are suggestions for daily yoga routines, information on proper diet, recipes, and alternative healing techniques.

MEDITATION FOR STARTERS *WITH CD*

Swami Kriyananda

Have you wanted to learn to meditate, but just never got around to it? Or tried "sitting in the silence" only to find yourself too restless to stay more than a few moments? If so, *Meditation for Starters* is just what you've been looking for—and with a companion CD, it provides everything you need to begin a meditation practice.

Filled with easy-to-follow instructions, beautiful guided visualizations, and answers to important questions on meditation, this book includes: what meditation is (and isn't); how to relax your body and prepare yourself for going within; and techniques for interiorizing and focusing the mind.

AWAKEN TO SUPERCONSCIOUSNESS

Swami Kriyananda

This popular guide includes everything you need to know about the philosophy and practice of meditation, and how to apply the meditative mind to resolve common daily conflicts in uncommon, superconscious ways.

Superconsciousness is the hidden mechanism at work behind intuition, spiritual and physical healing, successful problem solving, and finding deep and lasting joy.

HOW TO MEDITATE

A Step-by-Step Guide to the Art & Science of Meditation

Jyotish Novak

This clear and concise guidebook contains everything you need to start your practice. With easy-to-follow instructions, meditation teacher Jyotish Novak demystifies meditation—presenting the essential techniques so that you can quickly grasp them. Since it was first published in 1989, *How to Meditate* has helped thousands to establish a regular meditation routine. This newly revised edition includes a bonus chapter on scientific studies showing the benefits of meditation, plus all-new photographs and illustrations.

LIVING WISELY, LIVING WELL

Swami Kriyananda

Winner of the 2011 International Book Award for Best Self-Help: Motivational Title

Want to transform your life? Tap into your highest potential? Get inspired, uplifted, and motivated?

Living Wisely, Living Well contains 366 practical ways to improve your life—a thought for each day of the year. Each reading is warm with wisdom, alive with positive expectation, and provides simple actions that bring profound results. See life with new eyes. Discover hundreds of techniques for self-improvement.

THE BHAGAVAD GITA

According to Paramhansa Yogananda

Edited by his disciple, Swami Kriyananda

Based on the teachings of Paramhansa Yogananda, this translation of the Gita brings alive the deep spiritual insights and poetic beauty of the famous battlefield dialogue between Krishna and Arjuna. Based on the little-known truth that each character in the Gita represents an aspect of our being, it expresses with revelatory clarity how to win the struggle within between the forces of our lower and higher natures.

CRYSTAL CLARITY PUBLISHERS

Crystal Clarity Publishers offers additional resources to assist you in your spiritual journey including many other books, a wide variety of inspirational and relaxation music composed by Swami Kriyananda, and yoga and meditation videos. To see a complete listing of our products, contact us for a print catalog or see our website: www.crystalclarity.com

Crystal Clarity Publishers
14618 Tyler Foote Rd., Nevada City, CA 95959
TOLL FREE: 800.424.1055 or 530.478.7600 / FAX: 530.478.7610
EMAIL: clarity@crystalclarity.com

ANANDA WORLDWIDE

Ananda Sangha, a worldwide organization founded by Swami Kriyananda, offers spiritual support and resources based on the teachings of Paramhansa Yogananda. There are Ananda spiritual communities in Nevada City, Sacramento, Palo Alto, and Los Angeles, California; Seattle, Washington; Portland and Laurelwood, Oregon; as well as a retreat center and European community in Assisi, Italy, and communities near New Delhi and Pune, India. Ananda supports more than 140 meditation groups worldwide.

For more information about Ananda Sangha communities or meditation groups near you, please call 530.478.7560 *or visit www.ananda.org*

THE EXPANDING LIGHT

Ananda's guest retreat, The Expanding Light, offers a varied, year-round schedule of classes and workshops on yoga, meditation, and spiritual practice. You may also come for a relaxed personal renewal, participating in ongoing activities as much or as little as you wish. The beautiful serene mountain setting, supportive staff, and delicious vegetarian food provide an ideal environment for a truly meaningful, spiritual vacation.

For more information, please call 800.346.5350
or visit www.expandinglight.org